A HANDHOLDING GUIDE TO SHARE MARKET

A COURSE FOR STOCK MARKET

RAHUL ROY

Made with ♥ on the Notion Press Platform
www.notionpress.com

Contents

Foreword

About the Author:

Mr. Rahul Roy is an eminent Trader for more than a Decade. He is a SEBI Registered Research Analyst and took training and certification in Technical Analysis from IIT ISM DMS Dhanbad. He is also an AMFI Licensed MF Distributor. He was one of the Finalist in National level Trading Contest -Trade-a-Thon , held in the year 2022.His Qualification is M.A (Eng), CTET, B.ed, PGDCA. He has been taking many training sessions in both Online and Offline mode to create awareness in the field of Share Market.

Preface

Preface:

Hello Friends,

This book covers the Basic concepts of Share Market which is a pre-requisite for entering into the world of Stock Market. In this book I have compiled the most important concepts required for understanding the functionality of stock Market . It will surely assist you to become a successful Trader cum Investor. This book is a very precise version of all the fundamentals of Stock Market. One can complete the book in few days and start trading. So start learning and earning simultaneously! For any suggestion please write to me at- rahulroycv@gmail.com.

Disclaimer: Some parts are taken from open source available in Google. The Source has been mentioned wherever required.

"The key to trading success is emotional discipline.If intelligence were the key, there would be a lot more people making money trading... I know this will sound like a cliché, but the single most important reason that people lose money in the financial markets is that they don't cut their losses short." – Victor Sperandeo

Thanks

Rahul Roy

Prologue

TABLE OF CONTENT:

CHAPTER ONE

INTRO TO STOCK MARKET

STOCK MARKET:

The stock or Share market is a Galaxy of exchanges where securities like shares and bonds are bought and sold.

It helps companies raise money to fund operations by selling shares of stock, and it creates and sustains wealth for individual investors.

Companies raise money by selling shares to investors. These equity stakes are known as shares of stock. By listing shares for sale on the stock exchanges like NSE/BSE that make up the stock market, companies get access to the capital they need to operate and expand their businesses without having to take on loan or debt from Financial Institutions. In exchange for the privilege of selling stock to the public, companies are required to disclose information and give shareholders an ownership right on their businesses.

Investors benefit by exchanging their money for shares on the stock market. As companies put that money to work growing and expanding their businesses, investors reap the benefits as their shares of stock become more valuable over time, leading to capital gains. In addition, companies pay dividends to their shareholders as their profits grow.

The performances of individual stocks vary widely over time, but taken as a whole the stock market has historically rewarded investors with average annual returns of around 10 to 15 %, making it one of the most reliable ways of growing your money.

The daily movement of the prices of the shares are caused due to Demand and supply and share transfer by the Retail Investors , FII(Foreign Institutional Investors) , DII (Domestic Institutional Investors) , etc.

How to Invest in the Stock Market:

If you want to invest in the stock market, the process to get started is easier than you think:

- Decide what kind of account you want to open. From retirement savings to college savings, from short-term goals to long, there really is an investment account for everything.
- Open a brokerage account for example Zerodha/Upstox/Angel Broking/5Paisa/Icici /etc. When choosing a company, consider their fees and available investment options.
- Deposit money. To get started, you need to make an initial deposit (It can be as low as 500 rupees) .
- Choose your investments. Once your account is open, you can buy and sell securities. You can opt for individual stocks and bonds or mutual funds, index funds and exchange-traded funds (ETFs) that contain hundreds of individual securities.
- Purchase your investments. Once you've settled on what you want to buy, simply enter the ticker symbol in the buy field and indicate how many shares you want to buy.

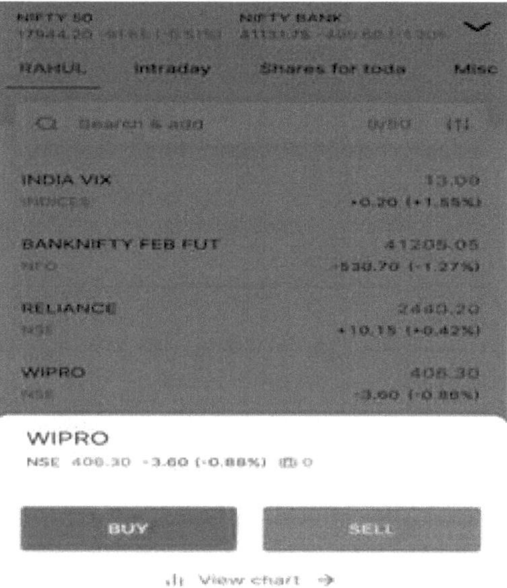

Just hover your mouse to the stock you want to buy and click Buy option. (Zerodha KITE MOBILE Terminal)

Select the quantity (Given 2 Qty), Price at which you want to buy (Also called Limit order) and click buy. Shares will be bought.

For selling Click on Sell button and follow the process.

What Is Traded On The Share Market?

There are many categories of financial instruments that are traded on the stock exchange. Some of these include:

Shares

A share represents a unit of equity ownership in a company. Shareholders are entitled to any profits that the company may earn in the form of dividends. They are also the bearers of any losses that the company may face.

Bonds

To undertake long term and profitable projects, a company requires substantial capital. One way to raise capital is to issue bonds to the public. These bonds represent a "loan" taken by the company. The bondholders become the creditors of the company and receive timely interest payments in the form of coupons. From the perspective of the bondholders, these bonds act as fixed income instruments, where they receive interest on their investment as well as their invested amount at the end of the prescribed period.

Mutual Funds

Mutual funds are professionally managed funds that pool the money of numerous investors and invest the collective capital into various financial securities. You can find mutual funds for a variety of financial instruments like equity, debt, or hybrid funds, to name a few.

Each mutual fund scheme issues units that are of a certain value similar to a share. When you invest in such funds, you become a unit-holder in that mutual fund scheme. When instruments that are part of that mutual fund scheme earn revenue over time, the unit-holder receives that revenue reflected as the net asset value of the fund or in the form of dividend payouts.

Derivatives

A derivative is a security that derives its value from an underlying security. This can have a wide variety such as shares, bonds, currency, commodities and more! The buyers and sellers of derivatives have opposing expectations of the price of an asset, and hence, enter into a "betting contract" with regards to its future price.

Types of Trading: An individual can trade in two different ways in the share market – delivery or intra-day.

What is Intraday Trading?

Intraday trading refers to the process of buying and selling shares on the same day. Hence, there will be no holding or transfer of shares to the Demat account. You can either buy first and sell at a profit or loss or sell first and buy at a profit or loss, all on the same day. In some cases, if you do not close (square off) your open position fifteen minutes before the market closing time, your broker may close it automatically against some fee.

Intraday traders usually set a target price before entering the trade. They also place a stop loss to exit automatically if the market reacts differently. Intraday traders enter the market to get quick profits.

What is Delivery Trading?

Delivery trading refers to the process of buying shares on one day and selling at a later date. Even BTST (Buy Today Sell Today) trades are also referred to as delivery trades. When you buy shares on day one, the shares are transferred to your account after two business days. Similarly, when you sell shares, they get debited from the trading account after two working days. Once you buy shares on delivery, you become the rightful owner of the shares, and you can sell them any time you want.

Like intraday traders, delivery traders also set the target before placing trades. However, since they hold the shares, they are in no hurry to close the trade on the purchase date.

CHAPTER TWO

INTRO TO THE CANDLESTICKS

Here are several vital components that make the price analysis intuitive to comprehend the candlestick's purpose.

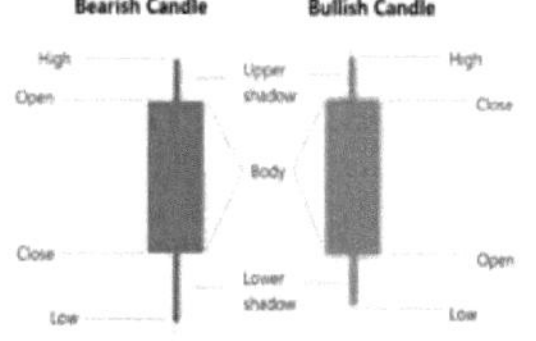

1st Candle- RED , 2nd Candle- GREEN

Candle Body

The body represents the open and close price of an asset. The open or close points' position depends on whether the candlestick and hence the price is bullish or bearish in a given period. In a bullish market, the close will be above the open and vice versa.

Candle Wick/Shadow

Each candlestick generally has two so-called shadows, or wicks, though this is not generally a rule. The shadows represent the high and low of a price for a given period. Thus, the upper shadow stands for the peak, and the lower shadow shows the lowest point touched by the price. Sometimes one of the shadows might be visible. It happens when the high or low coincides with the open or close.

Candle Color

The color of the body shows the direction of price movement. Usually, a green (or white) body suggests a price increase and a red (or black) body points to a price decline. You will most likely see green and red bodies on most platforms. Consequently, if the body is green, its upper limit will indicate the close price.

Some Imp. Candlestick Patterns:

While there are plenty of candlestick patterns, we'll list the most popular and reliable ones. Starting with bullish patterns, which show up after a downtrend and anticipate a reversal.

Here they are:

1. Hammer

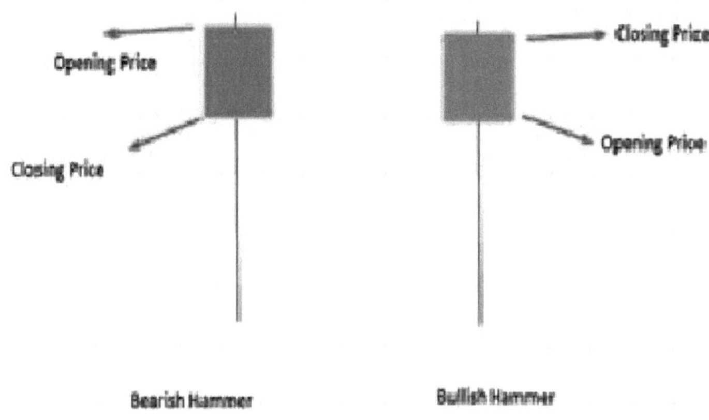

1st Candle- RED, 2nd Candle- GREEN

The hammer candlestick consists of a short body with a much longer lower shadow. As a rule, you will find it at the bottom of a downtrend. The pattern indicates that bulls resisted the selling pressure during a given period and pushed the price back up. While there may be hammer patterns with green and red candles, the former points to a stronger uptrend than red hammers.

2. Inverse Hammer

The inverse hammer is quite similar to the previously described pattern. It is different from the standard hammer in that it has a much longer upper shadow while the lower wick is very short. The pattern suggests a buying pressure, followed by bears' failed attempt to drag the price down. As a result, buyers come back with even stronger coercion and push prices higher.

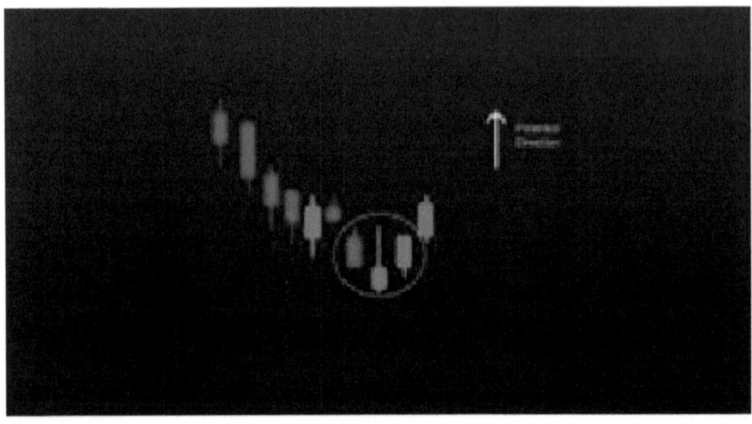

3. Bullish Engulfing

Unlike the previous two patterns, bullish engulfing is made up of two candlesticks. The first candle should be a short red body engulfed by a green candle, which is larger. While the second candle opens lower than the previous red one, the buying pressure increases, leading to a reversal of the downtrend.

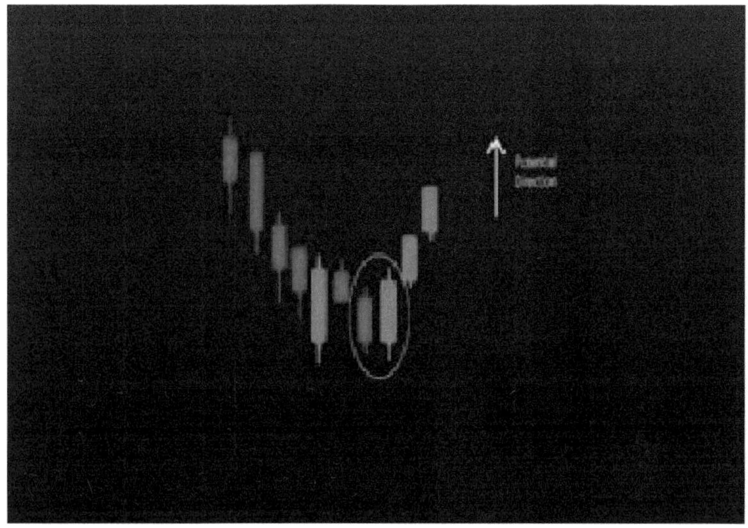

4. Piercing Line

Another two-candlestick pattern is the piercing line, which may show up at the bottom of a downtrend, at the support level, or during a pullback. The pattern consists of a long red candle that is followed by a long green candle. The critical aspect of this pattern is that there is a significant gap between the red candle's closing price and the green candle's open price. The fact that the green candle opens much higher points to buying pressure.

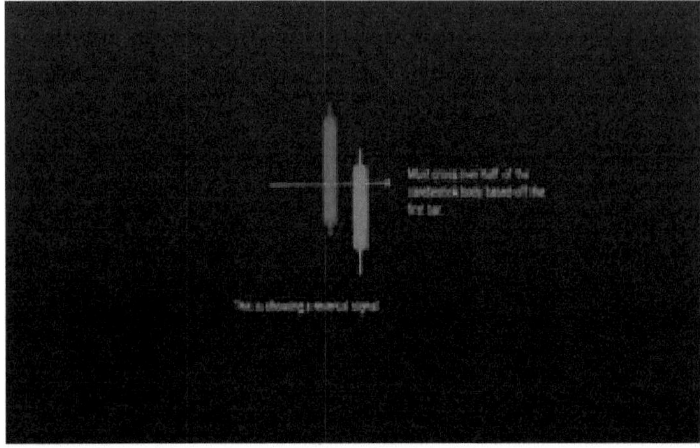

5. Morning Star

The morning star pattern is more complex because it comprises three candlesticks: a long red followed by a short-bodied candle and a long green. Usually, the middle candle will have no overlap with the longer ones. The morning start suggests that the first period's selling pressure is fading, and a bull market is forming.

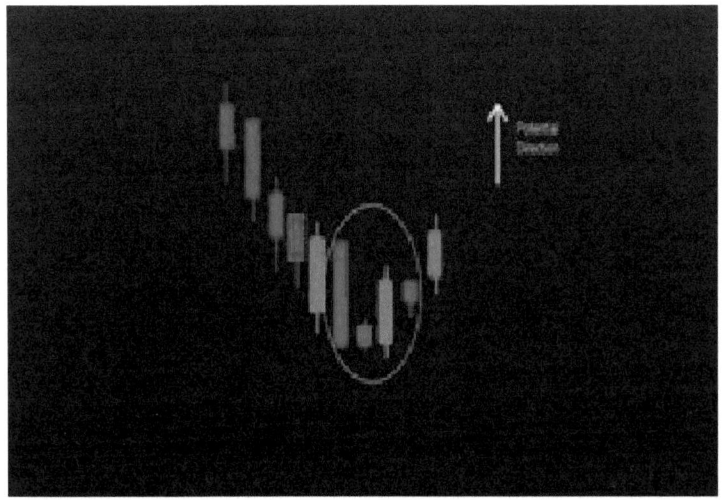

6. Hanging Man

The hanging man is the same pattern as the hammer, only inversed. Thus, it is formed by a green or red candlestick with a short body and a long lower shadow. It shows up at the end of an uptrend. It suggests a considerable sell-off during a given period, but bulls could temporarily push prices higher, after which they lose control.

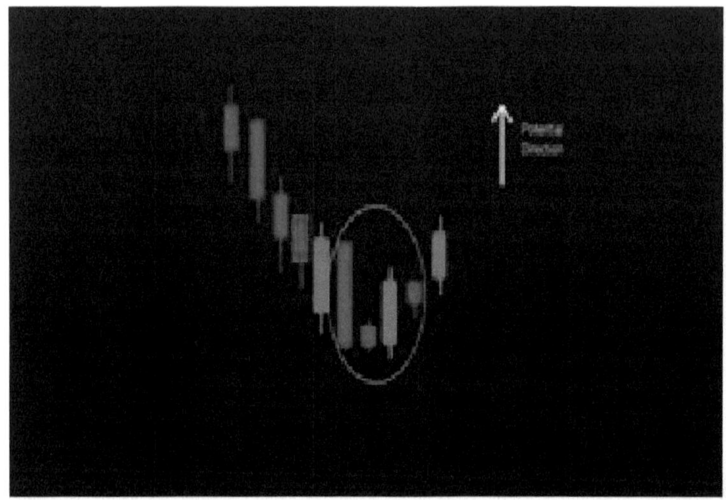

7. Shooting Star

The shooting star is the opposite of an inverted hammer. It consists of a red candle with a short body and a long upper shadow. Generally, the market will gap a bit higher on the candlestick opening and will surge to a local peak before closing just below the open. The body can sometimes be almost non-existent.

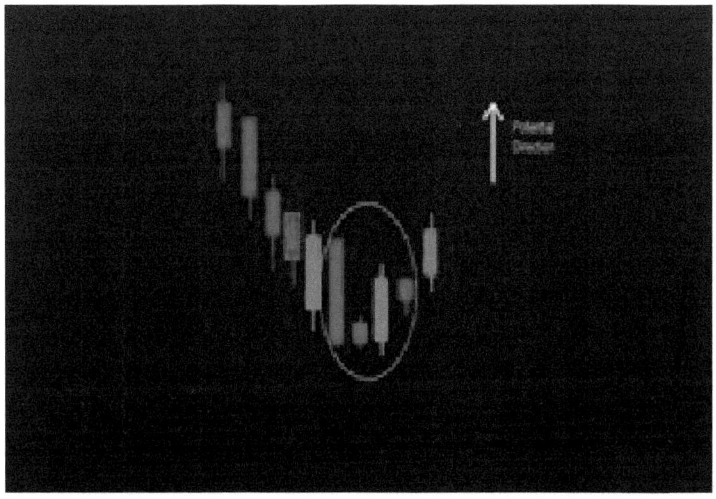

8. Evening Star

Again, the evening star is the inverse version of the bullish morning star, and it represents a three-stick pattern. It consists of a short-bodied candle that comes between a long green candle and a large red candle.

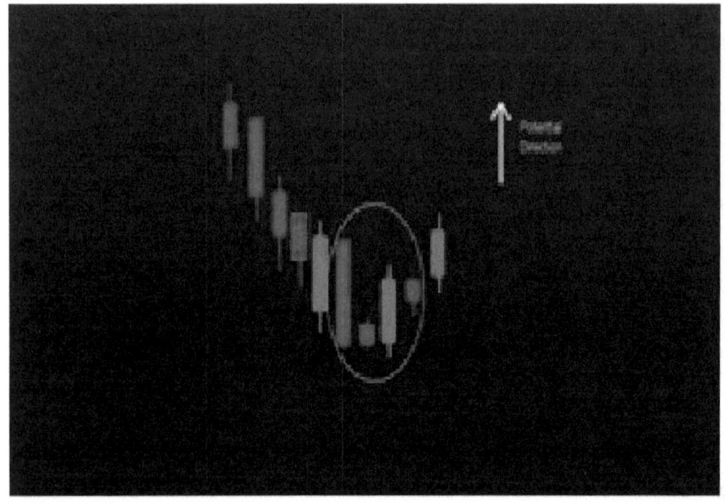

9. Dark Cloud Cover

The dark cloud cover pattern anticipates a bearish reversal. The pattern comprises two candlesticks – a red candle that opens above the previous green body and closes below its midpoint. It suggests that bears have taken control of the market, pushing prices lower. If the shadows of the candles are short, then traders could expect a strong downtrend.

Besides the bullish and bearish patterns that anticipate trend reversals, there are also candlestick patterns that are neutral or point to the continuation of a trend, be it bullish or bearish.

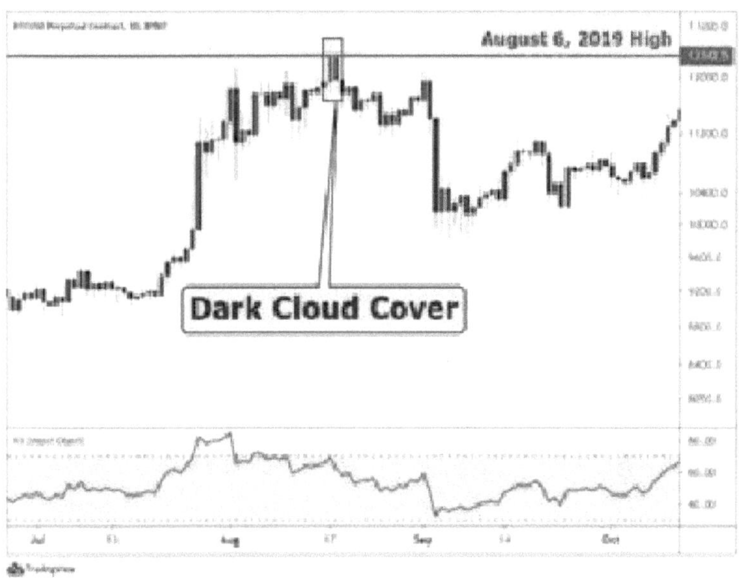

10. Doji

The Doji candlestick has an exceptionally small body and long shadows. While it is generally perceived as a trend continuation pattern, traders should be careful because it might also end up with a reversal. To avoid confusion, you should open a position a few candles after Doji when the situation becomes clear.

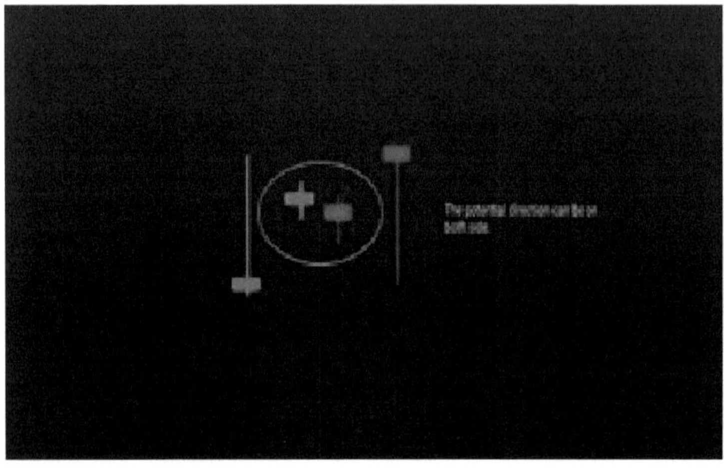

11. Spinning Top

Like Doji, the spinning top is a candlestick with a short body. However, the two shadows are of equal length, leaving the body right in the middle. This pattern also indicates indecision and may suggest a period of rest or consolidation after a significant rally or price decline.

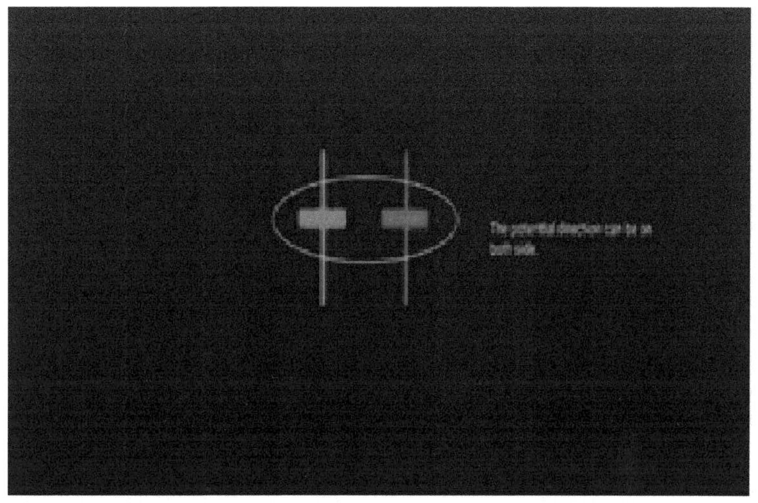

Source -Bybit.com

CHAPTER THREE

INTRO TO CHART PATTERN

1. Head and Shoulders:

This is a bullish and bearish reversal patterns which has a large peak in the middle and smaller peaks on the either sides.

Head and shoulders pattern is considered to be one of the most reliable reversal chart patterns.This pattern is formed when the prices of the stock rises to a peak and falls down to the same level from where it had started rising.Again the prices rises and form a peak higher than the last peak and again it declines to the original base.Prices again rise to form a third peak, which is lower than the second peak and from here it starts declining to the base level.

When the prices break the baseline with volume then bearish reversal takes place.

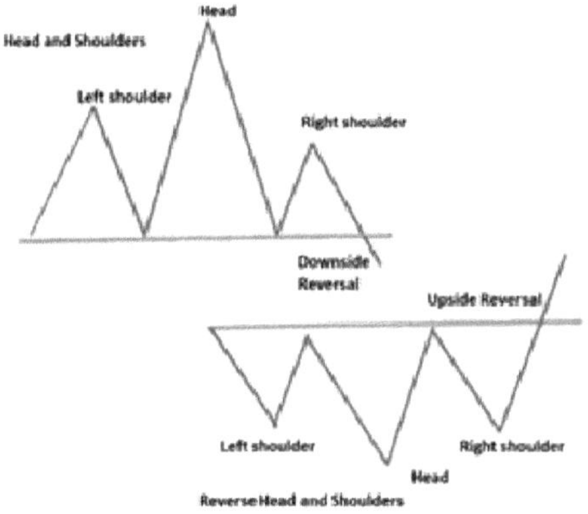

2. Double top:

A double top is another bearish reversal pattern that traders use a lot.

The stock price will form a peak and then retrace back to a level of support. It will then form a peak once more before reversing back from the prevailing trend.

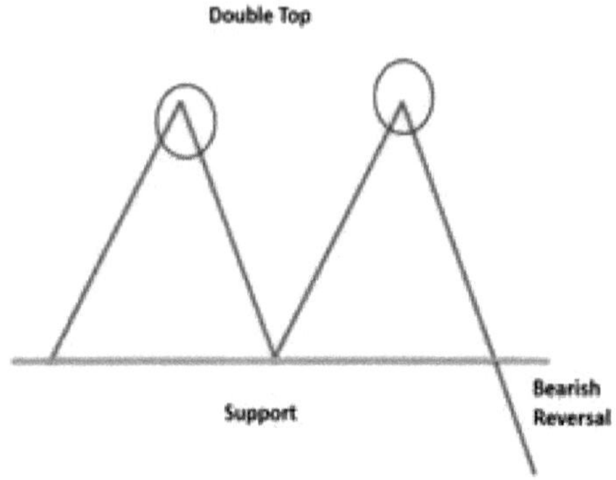

3. Double Bottom:

A double bottom is bullish reversal pattern that is totally opposite of double top.

The stock price will form a peak and then retrace back to a level of resistance. It will then form a peak once more before reversing back from the prevailing trend.

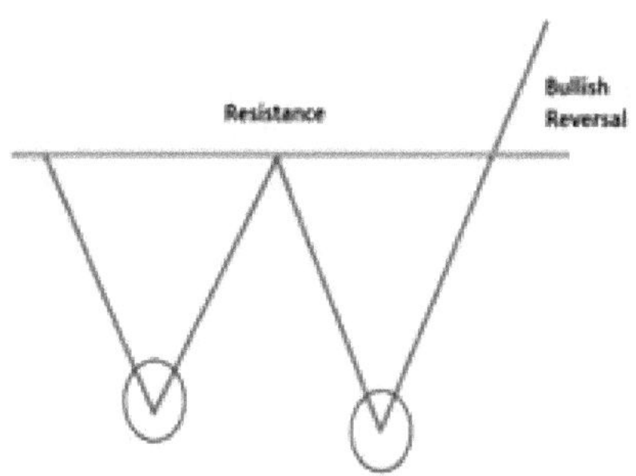

4. Cup and Handle:

A cup and handle is a bullish reversal chart pattern which resembles a cup and handle where the cup is in the shape of a "U" and the handle has a slight downward drift.

The cup appears similar to a rounding bottom chart pattern, and the handle is similar to a wedge pattern.The right-hand side of the pattern has low trading volume that may be as short as seven weeks or as long as 65 weeks.

5. Rounding Bottom:

This pattern is also known as the “saucer bottom” and is long-term reversal chart pattern.

Rounding Bottom shows that the stock is reversing from a downward trend towards an upward trend.

It can take any time from several months to years to form. It is very similar to the cup and handle, but the only difference is that there is no handle to the pattern.

6. *Wedges :*

Wedges are bullish and bearish reversal as well as continuation patterns which are formed by joining two trend lines which converge. It can be a rising wedge or a falling wedge.

Rising wedge occurs when the price of the stock is rising over a time whereas falling wedge occurs when the price of the stock is falling over a time.

Wedge pattern can be drawn by using trend lines and connecting the peaks and the troughs.

Once there is price breakout, there is a sharp movement of prices in either of the directions.

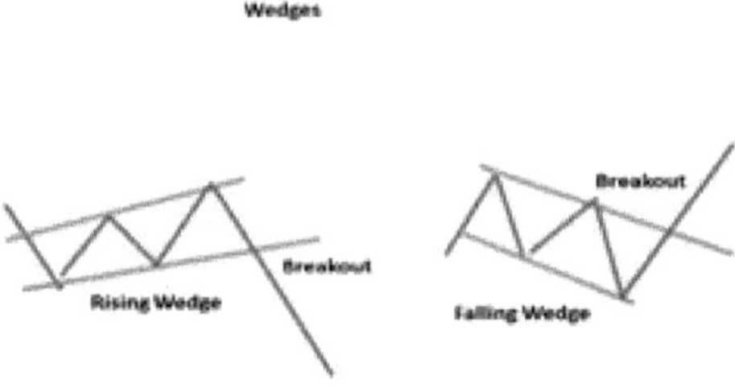

7. Pennants:

A pennant pattern or a flag pattern is created when there is a sharp movement in the stock either upward or downward.

This is followed by a period of consolidation that creates the pennant shape because of the converging lines.

Then a breakout movement occurs in the same direction as the big stock move. Pennants patterns are similar to flag patterns and tend to last between one and three weeks.At the initial stock movement there is a significant volume which is followed by weaker volume in the pennant section, and then rise in the volume at the breakout.

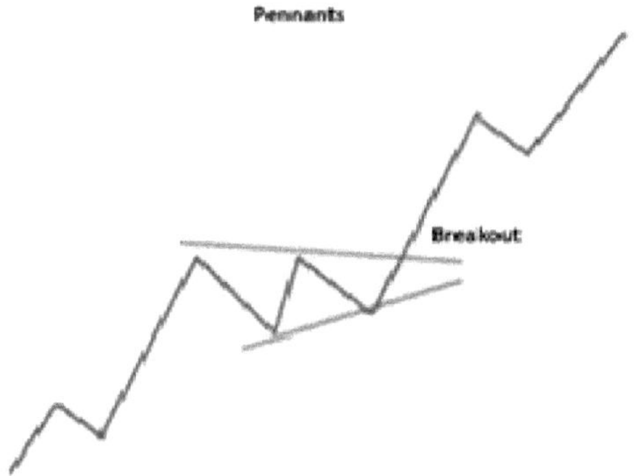

Source- Elearnmarkets.com

CHAPTER FOUR

INTRO TO MOVING AVERAGES

What are Moving Averages?

Before we move on to moving averages, let me refresh your memory about what are averages. An average is simply a representative figure, calculated by taking a sum of all data points and then dividing the sum by the number of data points. For instance, you know that on average you take 30 mins to reach your office. How did you come upon this number? You simply calculated an average based on the time you took to reach your office in the past. That's all!

Now let's come to the Moving average. Talking about the stock market, every day we see a different closing price of the stocks. So, how do we get to know the average market price of a stock and its general trend? This is where the moving averages come into the picture. The Moving average calculations consider the most recent number of data points (closing price of an asset). For example, for 5 days moving average, it will be continuously recalculated by taking the closing price of the recent 5 trading days. So, after every trading session, that day's closing price would be included, resulting in the exclusion of the oldest closing price from the previous day's data. This way the data points keep moving ahead every day and hence the name Moving Averages or Simple Moving Averages (SMA).

What is Exponential Moving Average?

EMA is a type of moving average. We can say that it is an extension of SMA. So, what's different about EMA? The recalculation remains the same. Additionally, weights are given to the prices. The recent data will be assigned more weight compared to the older data. This makes sense because more importance is given to the price which is already discounted based on recent news, events, etc. Hence, EMA tends to react quickly and give early signals than SMA. For all these reasons, EMA is widely used by technical analysts.

1. Simple Moving Average:

The SMA Is the simplest moving average that is obtained by adding the most recent data points set and then dividing the total by the number of time periods.

The SMA indicator is used for traders to generate signals of when to enter or exit the stock.

An SMA is a lagging indicator as it is based on the past price data for a given period that can be computed for different types of prices such as high, low, open, and close.

Traders use this indicator for determining buy, sell signals for securities and also helps to identify support and resistance zones.

For example, a stock trader wants to calculate the simple moving average for a stock by taking its closing price for the last five days.

The closing prices for the last five days are as follows: Rs.23, Rs.23.40, Rs.23.20, Rs.24, and Rs.25.50. The SMA is then calculated as follows:

SMA = (Rs.23 + Rs.23.40 + Rs.23.20 + Rs.24 + Rs.25.50) / 5

SMA = Rs.23.82

2. Exponential Moving Average (EMA):

EMA is the other type of moving average that gives more weight to the most recent price points and makes it more responsive to recent data points.

EMA is more responsive to recent price change when compared to the SMA as it applies the same weight to all price changes in the given specific period.

There are three steps involved when calculating EMA:

- First, we need to calculate the simple moving average for the specific period.
- Then we need to calculate the multiplier for weighing the exponential moving average.
- The last step involves the calculation of the current EMA by taking the period from the initial EMA until the most recent time period, using the price, multiplier, and the previous period's EMA value. The formula is:

Current EMA = [Closing Price – EMA (Previous Time Period)] x Multiplier + EMA (Previous Time Period)

3. Weighted Moving Average(WMA):

WMA is another type of moving average which traders use for generating trade direction and making a buy or sell decision.

It gives greater weightage to the recent data points and less weightage on past data points.

It is calculated by multiplying each point in the data set by a weighting factor.

Traders use the weighted average for generating trade signals. For example, when the prices are above the weighted moving average, then it signals that the trend is an uptrend.

But if the prices are below the weighted moving, then it indicates the trend is down.

4. Double Exponential Moving Average (DEMA):

DEMA is an improved version of EMA as it allocates more weight to the most recent data points.

It reduces lag results and is more responsive that helps short-term traders in spotting trend reversals quickly.

Since the DEMA line mimics the stock prices most closely, it is, therefore, most sensitive to the stock volatility. Changes in volatility are good indicators for a trend reversal, and hence, stock trades.

Bottomline:

Moving Average is mainly used for identifying the trend of any financial securities rather than giving trading signals as it is a lagging indicator. As with the other technical indicators, moving averages should also be used with other technical tools like price action or momentum indicators.

CHAPTER FIVE

TIPS AND TRICKS

MY PRINCIPLE(S) BEHIND THE EXECUTION OF TRADES:

My 1st Principle is to save the Initial Capital. My entire energy is channelized to protect my Capital during the days of trading.

As I believe MONEY SAVED IS MONEY EARNED. In this market if I don't loose money then ultimately I would make money.

My 2nd Principle is to choose the stocks for long term benefits and not merely for some days (In case of Delivery not Intraday) to generate maximum return. So I consider more on quality stocks and mostly market leaders.

My 3rd Principle is Proper diversification of the stocks.Try to take advantage of Banking sector, IT sector, FMCG, Tourism & Hospitality sector ,etc. As I believe in the rule - DON'T PUT ALL YOUR EGGS IN ONE BASKET

TRADE SETUP

I Follow 3 approaches for the trades which I execute-

1. *MARKET SENTIMENTS AND PSYCHOLOGY- To gauze the short term and long term view of the market like Bearishness or Bullishness (For this I use the data of Global markets , Option Chain and latest news updates)*
2. *FUNDAMENTAL ANALYSIS- To know the status of the company through SWOT analysis and also follow Bottom Up approach (Company-Industry-Economy). I use Bottom up approach because I had to basically give my best within few days.*

3. *TECHNICAL ANALYSIS- To catch the upcoming momentum and to locate entry and exit points. ALONG WITH THESE I FOLLOW A STRICT RISK IS TO REWARD RATIO OF MINIMUM 1:3*

Intraday trading tips for beginners

One of the most riskiest, yet profitable methods of stock trading is day trading. Also known as intraday trading, day trading involves purchasing and selling stocks within a single trading session. If you're interested in utilizing this strategy to make money from the stock market, then here are some basic intraday trading tips that you can use.

1. Pick the right stocks

The first and foremost thing that you should do when getting into day trading is selecting the right stock to buy. Not all stocks are good contenders for intraday trading. Since you would be buying and selling them within a trading session, you would need to choose stocks with high amounts of liquidity, which will make purchasing and selling that much easier. Large cap stocks and mid cap stocks are the best bet for day trading since they usually have high liquidity.

2. Set target prices for entry and exit

Once you've chosen the stock that you wish to trade in, the next step is to set target prices for both entry and exit. Going into a trade blindly without any targets is a recipe for disaster. Set a price at which you would like to buy the stock and stick to it, even if it means that you may not get a chance to buy the stock. Similarly, set a target at which you would like to sell the stock, even if it means that you might miss out on any further gains that the stock may or may not make.

3. Don't forget to set stop loss

The first thing that you should do right after purchasing the stock is to set a stop loss. This will allow you to prevent any significant losses if the stock were to move against your expectations. For instance, let's say that you buy a stock at Rs. 500, expecting it to go up. However, you place a stop loss at Rs. 490 as a safety net. Now, if the stock goes against your expectations and drops to Rs. 490, the stop loss will get triggered and your stock will be sold at a loss of Rs. 10. And you will be protected from any further downsides in the price as well.

4. Always go with the trend

This is one of the best intraday trading tips that you can follow. If the market trend is bullish, it is advisable to buy stocks. And if it is negative, it is advisable to short-sell stocks. It is never a good idea to hold a contrarian view of the market since it can backfire. For instance, many individuals short-sell stocks when the market is bullish expecting a reversal of the price. Such reversals happen rarely and few and far between.

5. Do not challenge the market:

Predicting the stock market is a tedious task. You will often make decisions regarding the intraday trading strategy you wish to adapt based on your market analysis. However, when you begin trading, the market may go in the opposite direction.

You must remember to refrain from challenging the market and getting fixated on your analysis during such scenarios. A better option is to sell your stock as soon as it reaches stop-loss level.

SOME TIPS:

Tip 1:

If you want to stay in this business, leave "hope at the door and put a stop loss".

Tip 2:

When you start trading (open a position), start looking for signs that you are wrong. If you see them, then get out before you hit the stop loss.

Tip 3:

Trading should be tiring, like working in a factory. If there is a guarantee in trading, it is: "excited traders drain their accounts".

Tip 4:

Don't jump into the "next hot thing." Develop your plan and follow it.

Tip 5:

You trade other merchants of non-existent goods. You have to take into account (feel) the psychology and emotions behind trading.

Tip 6:

Be aware of your own emotions. Irrational behavior is the downfall of every trader. If you shout in front of your computer begging for the price to move in your direction, you should ask yourself, “Is this rational?” Easy entry. Calm out. Put stops. Don’t shout.

Tip 7:

Don’t worry too much – excitement increases the risk as it obscures the mind.

Tip 8:

Don’t trade too much – be patient and wait for 3-5 good trades.

Tip 9:

If you come to trade with the idea of making “big money”, you are doomed. This mental attitude is the reason for blowing up most accounts.

Tip 10:

Don’t focus on money. Focus on the proper execution of commercial operations. If entering and exiting the trade is rational, the money will take care of itself.

CHAPTER SIX

OPTION TRADING (BUYING PART)

Options trading is how investors can speculate on the future direction of the overall stock market or individual securities, like stocks or bonds. Options contracts give you the choice—but not the obligation—to buy or sell an underlying asset at a specified price by a specified date.

- **Derivative.**Options are what's known as a derivative, meaning that they derive their value from another asset. Take stock options, where the price of a given stock dictates the value of the option contract.
- **Call option and put option.**A call option gives you the opportunity to buy a security at a predetermined price by a specified date while a put option allows you to sell a security at a future date and price.
- **Strike price and expiration date.**That predetermined price mentioned above is what's known as a strike price. Traders have until an option contract's expiration date to exercise the option at its strike price.
- **Premium.**The price to purchase an option is called a premium, and it's calculated based on the underlying security's price and values.
- **Intrinsic value and extrinsic value.**Intrinsic value is the difference between an option contract's strike price and current

price of the underlying asset. Extrinsic value represents other factors outside of those considered in intrinsic value that affect the premium, like how long the option is good for.

- **<u>In-the-money and out-of-the-money.</u>**Depending on the underlying security's price and the time remaining until expiration, an option is said to be in-the-money (profitable) or out-of-the-money (unprofitable).

Buy Call

Buying or "Going Long" on a Call is a strategy that must be devised when the investor is bullish on the market direction moving up in the short term.

A Long Call Option is the simplest way to benefit if the investor believes that the market will make an upward move. It is the most common choice among first-time investors. "Being Long" on a Call Option means the investor will benefit if the underlying Stock/Index rallies. However, the risk is limited on the downside if the underlying Stock/Index makes a correction.

Investor View: Bullish on the Stock / Index.

Risk: Limited to the premium paid.

Reward: Unlimited.

Breakeven: Strike Price + premium paid.

Illustration

E.g. Nifty is currently trading @ 5500. Investor is expecting the markets to rise from these levels. So buying Call Option of Nifty having Strike 5500 @ premium 50 will benefit the investor when Nifty goes above 5550.

Strategy	Stock/Index	Type	Strike	Premium Outflow
Buy Call	NIFTY (Lot size 50)	Buy CALL	5500	50

The Payoff Schedule and Chart for the above is shown below.

Payoff Schedule

NIFTY @ Expiry	Net Payoff (₹)
5200	-2500
5300	-2500
5400	-2500
5500	-2500
5550	0
5600	2500
5700	7500
5800	12500
5900	17500

14000 12000 10000 8000 6000 4000 2000 0 -2000 -4000

CALL BUYING

PUT

STRADDLE

CHAPTER SEVEN

TERMINOLOGIES IN SHARE MARKET

A

Arbitrator

An arbitrator is an investor who is trying to capitalize on market inefficiencies such as market volatility, price, and dividends.

Ask

The lowest price at which someone is willing to sell the security.

American-Style Option

An options contract wherein you can exercise the contract at any time between the purchase date and the expiration date.

At-the-money

An at-the-money option is an option that would lead to zero cash flow if it were exercised immediately. An option is said to be "at the money" when the current price equals the strike price.

B

Bear Market

A market in which stock prices are falling.

Bearish View

A bearish view is a trend in the financial market that sees a downward trajectory in stock prices, foreseeing general loss.

Bid

The highest price a buyer is willing to pay for a stock.

Block Deal

Block trade is a trade that contains a quantity greater than or equal to 500,000 or a value greater than or equal to Rs. 5 crores and is executed through the Block Deal window. It is allowed for 35 minutes in trading hours between 9.15 AM and 9.50 AM.

Bonds

A bond is a negotiable certificate evidencing indebtedness. A debt security is generally issued by a company, municipality, or government agency. A bond investor lends money to the issuer and in exchange, the issuer promises to repay the loan amount on specified maturity date. The issuer usually pays the bondholder periodic interest payments over the life of the loan.

Bull Market

A market in which stock prices are rising.

Bullish View

A bullish view is a trend in the financial market that sees an upward trajectory in stock prices, foreseeing general gains.

Basis

It is defined as the difference between the spot price of the security and the relative price of its underlying futures contract.

Bear Spread

Bear Spread is an options trading strategy used when the underlying asset's price is bearish. In this strategy, a trader purchases a contract with a higher strike price and sells a contract with a lower strike price with the same expiration date.

Bull Spread

Bull Spread is a strategy that options traders use when they try to make a profit from an expected rise in the price of the underlying asset. In this strategy, an option at a lower strike price is bought and one at a higher price is sold with the same expiry date.

C

Capital Market

A marketplace that acts as a channel between suppliers of capital and those who want that capital for the growth of their business is called the Capital Market. It comprises both primary and secondary markets. Stock market and bond market are the 2 most common capital markets.

Cash/Equity Market

A cash market is a market where securities are purchased and received at the point of sale.

Churning

Churning is a practice of illegal and excessive trading to gain commission/profit in a customer's account without considering their investment goals.

Commodities

Commodities are tangible goods or services resulting from the process of production

Commodities Market

Commodities Market is a marketplace for investors who want to trade in precious metals, energy, natural gas, crude oil, spices and many others. Under the Forward Markets Commission, 22 commodity exchanges have been set up in India.

Contra Funds

An equity mutual fund where the fund manager invests majorly in companies that aren't performing well in the short term. This is done with anticipation that these stocks will be profitable in the long run.

Currencies

Notes and coins that are the 'current' medium of exchange in a country are called Currencies.

Cyclical Stocks

Companies whose stocks are sharply impacted by the changes (ups and downs) in an economy are called Cyclical Stocks.

Call Option

An option which gives the holder the right, but not the obligation, to buy a stock at a specified price within a specified time. Calls are purchased by investors who expect a price increase.

Clearing Margin

It is a financial security to ensure clearing members that the client will perform on their open futures and options contracts. As an investor or trader, you need to maintain the clearing margin with your broker so that they can guarantee the completion of the transaction.

Contract Month

The month in which futures contracts are settled either by making or accepting delivery is known as Contract Month. Also known as delivery month.

Covered Call Option Writing

In this trading strategy, the trader holds on to a long position of a security and simultaneously writes a call option on the same security to gain profits in the form of premiums.

Customer Margin

In the futures industry, Customer Margin is the financial guarantee required from both buyers and sellers of the futures contracts as well as sellers of the options contracts to ensure fulfillment of contractual obligations.

D

Day Order

An order that can be executed anytime during the market hours of the same day is known as a Day Order.

Debentures

Bonds issued by a company bearing a fixed rate of interest usually payable on specific dates and principal amount repayable on a particular date on redemption are called Debentures.

Debt Instruments

A debt instrument is an asset that entities use to raise capital or to generate investment income. It is a fixed-income asset to the investors where they get interest payments at regular intervals.

Debt Market

A marketplace in which debt market securities such as bonds, government bonds, certificates of deposits, debentures, commercial papers, etc. are bought and sold. It is also known as a Bond Market.

Demerger

It is a business strategy in which a corporation or a business is broken down or split into small businesses to operate on their own, sell, or be liquidated.

Derivatives Market

Financial market for financial instruments such as futures contracts or options whose value is derived from their underlying assets is known as the Derivatives Market. Only F&O are legally traded on exchanges and the others are traded on the Over-the-counter Market.

Diversified Equity Funds

A kind of fund that invests in companies regardless of their size and sector with an aim to maximize gains for investors is known as Diversified Equity Funds. For example - ULIPs and SIPs.

Domestic Institutional Investors

Indian investors who invest their money in the Indian financial markets are known as Domestic Institutional Investors (DIIs). For example - shareholders in the Indian stock market

Deep Discount Bonds

Also known as zero-coupon bonds, Deep Discount Bonds are debt instruments purchased at a nominal face value, and the total value of the investment is borne at the time of maturity.

Derivative

Financial contracts that earn their value from that of the underlying asset are known as derivatives.

E

Equity

Equity refers to the value that would be returned to a company's shareholders if all of the assets were liquidated and all of the company's debts were paid off.

Equity Index

It's a weighted average of the stocks used to measure how to perform the stocks are performing in the market.

Exchange-Traded Fund (ETF)

An exchange-traded fund (ETF) is a type of security that tracks an index, sector, commodity, or other asset and can be purchased or sold on a stock exchange the same way a regular stock can.

Equity Options

Equity options are a form of derivative where shares/stocks are the underlying assets.

European Options

A European option is a version of an options contract that limits execution to its expiration date.

Exercise

In options trading, "to exercise" means to put into effect the right to buy or sell the underlying security that is specified in the options contract.

Expiration Date

The option expiration date is the last day on which the option is valid, post which it ceases to exist. It's the deadline for deciding whether to exercise the option or let it expire. In India, generally, the monthly options contracts expire on the last Thursday of the expiry month and weekly options contracts expire on every Thursday of the week.

Expiration Time

The expiration time is the precise date and time at which derivatives contracts cease to trade and any obligations or rights come due or expire.

Exposure Margin

In addition to the Initial/SPAN® margin, the exposure margin is also collected in the F&O segment to protect the positions. Exposure margins regarding index futures and index option sell positions are 3% of the notional value. For futures on individual securities and sell positions in options on individual securities, the exposure margin is higher at 5% or 1.5 standard deviations of the logarithmic returns of the stock (in the underlying cash market) over the last six months period. It is applied to the notional value of a position.

Extrinsic Value

Extrinsic value is the difference between the market price of an option (premium)and its intrinsic price.

F

Forward Price

The cost of delivering an underlying asset, financial derivative, or currency to the buyer of a forward contract at a predetermined date is known as the Forward Price. It is based on an underlying financial asset's spot price, which includes carrying charges like interest, forgone costs, etc.

Funds Available

A sum of money available for an investor/trader in his account to invest/trade. Includes withdrawable funds and sale credit (Sell proceeds- Margin for sale)

Futures Market

A market in which futures contracts are bought and sold for delivery on a predetermined date is known as the Futures Market.

Forward Contract

In a forward contract, two parties agree to do a trade at some future date, at a stated price and quantity. No money changes hands at the time the deal is signed.

Futures Contracts

Futures Contracts are derivative instruments in which one party agrees with another party to buy or sell an asset at a predetermined price at some point in the future.

G

Gamma Hedging

Gamma Hedging is a strategy that helps to eliminate the risk formed by the underlying security's sudden and aggressive movements.

Gold ETFs

Gold ETFs (Exchange Traded Funds) is an investment tool that is based on the domestic price of physical gold. 1 unit of this ETF equals 1 gram of 99.5% pure gold. Like other ETFs, gold ETFs are listed in both NSE (National Stock Exchange of India Limited) and BSE (Bombay Stock Exchange) and can be bought and sold at market prices, just like any other regular stock.

Goods Till Triggered (GTT) Order

GTT orders are executed if the market price of the stock reaches the trigger price (predetermined limit price) before the expiry of the GTT order.

Government Securities

Government securities include investment products offered by a governmental body. They are government debt issuances that guarantee the full repayment of invested principal on the maturity of the security and periodic interest payments until then. They are also called G-secs or Gilt Funds.

H

Haircut

In financial terms, the difference between an asset's market value and the loan amount is known as a Haircut.

Hybrid Funds

Mutual fund schemes that invest in various asset classes such as equity, debt, bonds, and more are Hybrid Funds.

I

Immediate or Cancel (IOC) Order

An IOC Order is the one in which an order to buy or sell a security must be executed immediately and if any portion of the order is not executed, then the order must be canceled.

Intraday Trading

Intraday Trading refers to buying and selling securities on a stock exchange on the same day.

In-the-money

An option is said to be In-the-money whenever the buyer is in profit at particular spot price of underlying securities. For call option, it is when the spot price is higher than the strike price. For put option, it is when the spot price is lower than the strike price.

Initial Margin

For derivatives, Initial margin requirements are based on 99% value at risk over a two-day time horizon, applying the SPAN.

Intrinsic Value of an Option

The intrinsic value of an option is defined as the amount, by which an option is in the money, or the immediate exercise value of the option when the underlying position is marked-to-market.

Initial Public Offering (IPO)

An initial public offering (IPO) refers to the process of offering shares of a private corporation to the public in a new stock issuance for the first time. An IPO allows a company to raise equity capital from public investors.

L

Limit Order

An order where you set a price at which you want to buy/sell a security (limit price) is known as a Limit Order.

Long Position

A long position means that you are buying an asset speculating that the asset will increase in value

Long Hedge (Futures)

A long hedge is one where a long position is taken on a futures contract. A hedger uses when an asset is expected to be bought in the future. Alternatively, it can be used by a speculator who anticipates that the price of a contract will increase.

Lot Size

Lot size refers to the number of underlying securities in one contract. The lot size is determined keeping in mind the minimum contract size requirement at the time of introduction of derivative contracts on a particular underlying. For example, if shares of XYZ Ltd are quoted at Rs.1000 each and the minimum contract size is Rs.2 lacs, then the lot size for that particular scrips stands to be 200000/1000 = 200 shares i.e. one contract in XYZ Ltd. covers 200 shares.

M

MF SIP

Mutual Fund SIP is an investment strategy wherein an investor needs to invest the same amount of money in a particular mutual fund at every stipulated time(weekly/monthly/quarterly,etc.)

Margin

Margin is the money borrowed by an investor from the broker to purchase shares.

Margin Pledge

Margin Pledge means using your existing securities in your Demat account as collateral to avail extra margin.

Margin Trading

It is known as Margin Trading, when a trader can buy shares worth more than the funds available in his trading account.

Market Order

An order to buy/sell a security at the prevailing market price is known as a Market Order.

Money Market

Financial instruments with a maturity of 1 year or less and high liquidity such as commercial papers and treasury bills are traded in the Money Market.

N

NFO (New Funds Offer)

An NFO is a new fund offering launched by an asset management company (AMC) to raise capital from the market to invest in securities. Click here to know more about NFO.

O

Open Position

Open Position is an established or entered trade that is yet to be closed with an opposing trade.

Order

An order is an instruction given by the investor to a broker or brokerage firm to buy or sell a security on his/her behalf.

Order Book

An order book is an electronic list that details the buy and sell orders of a specific security or any financial instrument. It includes executed, pending, canceled, and rejected orders.

Over-the-counter Market

It is a financial market where products are traded over the counter, which means the two parties enter into a contract and agree on how it will be settled in the future.

Options Contracts

An option contract is a financial contract that gives an investor a right to either buy or sell an asset at a predetermined price by a specific date. However, it also entails a right to buy, but not an obligation.

Out-of-the-money

An out-of-the-money option is an option that would lead to negative cash flow if it were exercised immediately. A Call option is out-of-the-money when the current price stands at a level that is less than the strike price. In the case of a Put, the Put is said to be out of money if the current price is above the strike price.

P

Penny Stocks

Stocks with very small market capitalization are largely illiquid, and trade at extremely low prices are called Penny Stocks. These are often traded on a smaller exchange.

Primary Market

A segment of the capital market where new securities are issued and sold for the first time by a company is known as the Primary Market.

Put Option

A put option is a contract that gives the holder the right to sell a stock at a stated price within a fixed time period. Put options are purchased by those who think a stock may decline in price.

R

Robo Order

Robo Order is a multi-leg order in which securities automatically get bought or sold when the trigger price/target price is reached.

S

SIP

A systematic investment plan involves investing a consistent sum of money regularly into the same security or basket of securities.

Secondary Market

The Secondary Market, also known as the Aftermarket, is the financial market where previously issued financial instruments like stocks, bonds, futures and options are traded.

Security Holdings

Security Holdings are the securities held/traded till the previous trading day (T-1) within the portfolio of an investor for the delivery product.

Short Position

A short position is when you sell an asset by aiming to make a profit when an asset's price decreases.

Short Selling

Short Selling is when shares are sold after borrowing from the owner with the help of a brokerage and selling them at a market price with the hope that the prices will fall.

Sovereign Gold Bonds (SGB)

Sovereign Gold Bonds(SGB) is a form of securities provided and guaranteed by the Government of India and issued by the Reserve Bank of India. These bonds are issued in denominations of 1 gram onwards with 1 gm being the minimum and 4 kg being the maximum subscription limit for individual investors.

Stop Loss Order

The order in which you buy/sell a stock once a specific price is reached, thus reducing your chances of loss on a security position is known as a Stop Loss Order. It is of 3 types - Stop Loss Market Order, Stop Loss Limit Order and Trailing Stop Loss Order.

SPAN Margin

The initial margin for the F&O segment is calculated on a portfolio (a collection of futures and option positions) based approach. The margin calculation is carried out using software called – SPAN® (Standard Portfolio Analysis of Risk). SPAN® generates about 16 different scenarios by assuming different values to the price and volatility. For each of these scenarios, the possible loss that the portfolio would suffer is calculated.

THANK YOU AND WISH YOU A HAPPY TRADING CUM INVESTMENT JOURNEY AHEAD.

THANK YOU AND WISH YOU A HAPPY TRADING CUM INVESTMENT JOURNEY AHEAD.

"I will tell you how to become rich. Close the doors. Be fearful when others are greedy. Be greedy when others are fearful." – By Warren Buffett

Printed by Libri Plureos GmbH in Hamburg,
Germany